The Snarky Gardener's Veggie Growing Guide

Create Organic Abundance By Embracing Your Garden's Wild Side

By Don Abbott

Donald K Abbott

The Snarky Gardener

Acknowledgements

Carol Grzeschik (a.k.a. The Snarky Girlfriend)

- for her creation of all the sketches in this book and for putting up with my ego

Kara Whaley

- for the picture used on the front cover and the others featured throughout the book

Kora Sadler and the Writers Group

- for building a place where people who are as strange I am can gather and offer encouragement to each other

Table of Contents

Introduction

I started out knowing next to nothing about gardening.

Almost a decade ago, I became an accidental gardener. Returning to my native Ohio after a five year stint in Florida (three hurricanes in four months was just too much for me), I was living in a rural duplex. My landlord came by one day to ask if I wanted a garden since he was already out tilling for other tenants. "Uh, sure, I guess," was my answer. Not exactly a strong commitment, but I figured, "What the heck. It'll give me something to do." The only garden experience I really had was recollections of my parents tending our garden, with us children mostly on weeding and poop spreading patrol.

My first garden was fine (for a while).

With faded childhood memories, I began in earnest, planting the newly prepared soil after a few trips to local garden shops. Purchasing seeds and starts of familiar vegetables (tomatoes, peppers, onions, peas, beans, squash, pumpkins, broccoli, and even turnips), my garden filled out in no time. That is when the "fun" began.

Then reality set in.

The five hundred square feet of reclaimed goldenrod and black raspberry clay-dominated land soon started fighting back. Weeds popped up, soil dried out, some plants grew poorly. All the weeding chores of my youth came back to bite me (literally—brambles and thistles are very, very pokey). I had to add fencing to keep out my newfound friends (those cold blooded, pea-eating, predatory bunnies), which of course found ways of getting around as hungry herbivores are bound to do. My first garden was a lot of work, but it also gave me the great feeling of accomplishment. Some veggies grew easily (yeah, green beans), so at least I had something to show for my efforts besides a sore back, scratches, and less money.

I've been where you are now.

I've spun this story of woe not to get sympathy (though that would be nice), but to show you that I've been where you are going. With all the conflicting information out there on the Interwebs and what not, growing your own vegetables may seem daunting. I've learned a LOT over the last ten years. With my advice, your first (or next) time out in the garden will be successful, cutting down on the mistakes many gardeners make.

I decided to write this book for Ohio, because that's where I have built my experience—though much of this information does apply to other temperate climates. USDA Plant Hardiness Zones http://planthardiness.ars.usda.gov/PHZMWeb/ let a gardener know what kind of plants they can grow. Most of Ohio is considered Zone 5 or 6. The number indicates how many frost-free months are available for a specific zip code. For example, based on my last average frost date of April 30 and my first average frost date of October 23 (almost 6 months), I am Zone 6a here in Kent, Ohio. When buying plants, especially perennials, make sure to check the zones to make sure you aren't planting something that won't survive our fun, yet tough, Ohio winters.

Here are some vegetable growing benefits:

1. Your garden can be your own backyard grocery store.
2. Producing your own food is one of the most rebellious acts you can take. Imagine the gall of people trying to create food out of thin air (and soil, water, sunlight, etc.).
3. Gives you a common subject to talk about with others (happens to me at work all the time).
4. You can give vegetables away to your neighbors and co-workers (it's called "building social capital").
5. You know how your food is raised and handled.
6. Reconnection with nature.
7. You'll have food to trade for other things you want.
8. You can enter your vegetables into fairs for bragging rights.
9. Great excuse to get more exercise.
10. You can name all your plants ("Morning, Fred. Howdy, Marge!").
11. It's scientifically proven that working with soil has mental and physical health benefits.
12. People at work can ask you questions about gardening (bonus points with the boss).

Learn about permaculture in your garden

Along my gardening journey, I discovered a new technique of designing gardens called "permaculture." Short for "permanent culture," this science uses natural patterns for its designs. Many common gardening practices fight what happens naturally. We till the soil, spray chemicals, plant the same exact crops in long straight lines, and remove all weeds leaving just bare soil. Who else besides humans does that? Why use your resources (time, money, energy) that could be used somewhere else (like napping)? As we take this journey together, you'll see permaculture applied in easy and straightforward ways to make your gardening efforts easier and sustainable.

Grow Food Now!

As I wrote this book, I concluded that I truly believe **EVERYONE** should grow food. Not all of their own food, since that's really hard, but *something*. Even herbs on your windowsill count (have you seen herb prices at the grocery store?). The very act of producing your own food gives you a special understanding of how nature works. Watching plants grow up from little tiny seeds to over 12 feet tall will sometimes make you realize how incredible life really is. Just don't get too attached to your plants, since you'll probably eat them in the future. It's not easy to consume your friends.

The best time to start growing your own food? Right now (even if there's 3 feet of snow outside). Plan now instead of throwing together a "last-minute middle-of-May" garden. It's a recipe for disaster I've seen repeated time and time again. By absorbing the material presented in the following chapters, you will have a deeper understanding of veggie production and all that it entails. If my advice keeps you from buying plants you shouldn't or digging unnecessary holes, it's well worth the price of admission.

Bonus:

Here's one more enticement to give this book a try. Go to http://thesnarkygardener.com/veggie-growing-guide to sign up for my FREE downloadable gardening PDF. It has fifty vegetables listed by how easy they are to grow, starting with beans at #1 and ending with parsnips (a relative of the carrot) at #50. It's a useful tool for any gardener—especially those just getting started.

Chapter 1 – Let's Grow Some Veggies

Growing food at its basic level seems easy to accomplish. Dig some soil, sow some seeds, plant some starts, and wait until you can eat your delicious rewards. But somewhere between planting and harvesting is where many go astray. Life takes over and keeps you from the garden for a week or two, or a month. The next time you actually interact with your garden, the weeds are 10 feet tall and your tomatoes are lying on the ground ("Help me!"). Or, there's a rainstorm and 6 inches of water pours onto your plot in a few hours and swamps everything you planted the day before. Or, there's a late last frost in the spring and the tomatoes and peppers you just planted are now blacker than burnt toast. Stupid nature!

There is, of course, a lot of science behind growing vegetables. But at the individual level, it's much more an artistic endeavor. Think of your garden as a blank canvas, and your seeds, plants, tools, knowledge, and experience as your materials. You want to design a successful garden starting now so you can plan ahead and be ready for any challenges as the season goes on. Nature makes gardening an art, as living things and weather are variable. While humans try to tame the wild, it sometimes makes more sense to take advantage of Mother Nature's tendencies. So soak up the information written here (and the Internet and other books and library talks and gardening groups), and strive to be a "Food Growing Artist" who can adapt to any situation.

What kind of skills and information do you need to be the best gardener on your block? First, you need in-depth knowledge of all the flora at your disposal. That's what Chapter 2 is all about. I will go through the primary vegetable families and their inherent strengths and weaknesses. For example, did you know most animals (including deer) will not eat garlic or onions? I've heard stories where people grow garlic around fruit trees and other vulnerable crops to deter deer from even going near them. Think about all the ways these could be deployed, even if you look out every morning to see deer herds as far as the eye can see.

Another skill you need to develop is understanding how our wonderful temperate seasons affect your growing activities. Did you know you can plant some vegetables outside as early as mid-March in Ohio? This fact alone blew me away when I started growing food. Based on childhood memories, I thought all gardening activity started on Memorial Day weekend and ended in late September. Truth be told, I have gathered salad greens on Christmas Day from the backyard. Nine months instead of four— pretty cool—and the subject of Chapter 8.

This book's goal is for you to make good choices for your unique situation. One size definitely doesn't fit all. What's important to one person doesn't matter to another. So, one question you need to ask yourself is "What do I want from my garden?" Some people want a fashion plate (is that a thing?), where neighbors will exclaim, "Wow, that's the most beautiful garden I've ever seen." Neat freaks want an orderly garden, with perfectly straight rows and bare and weedless soil. Some gardeners want (or need) to produce as much food for their families as possible for cost, health, and independence reasons. Then there are those who want to grow little known exotic plants for bragging rights. And, of course, some are looking for production with the least amount of work (like the Snarky Gardener). All of these maximize different attributes (beauty, order, production, extreme plants, laziness). Maximizing one parameter creates suboptimal results for other attributes. For example, it's difficult to be lazy and have no weeds.

"Question Everything" – Albert Einstein

Two of the best skills the modern day gardener can have are curiosity and asking the right questions. At my job as an applications developer, I've been fortunate to attend "Question Thinking" training. This is summed up in the book *Change Your Questions, Change Your Life* by Marilee Adams, which I highly recommend for anyone who wants to improve their life. Asking the right question can change your perspective in ways you can't imagine. The question that started me on my gardening journey was, "Could I grow enough food to totally feed me and my family?" After doing the calculations and discovering they haven't invented bacon plants, I realized raising one hundred percent of my food was a tough objective. So then I asked, "How much of my food could I grow?" Even if the answer is 5 percent, it's something. Growing your own food makes you appreciate it in ways that buying food from the store (even the "organic" ones) will never do.

Other questions that have changed my thinking were, "What is this weed?" and "Is it edible?" Instead of pulling my weeds all willy nilly and cursing their very existence, I now enjoy eating them in salads or using them as mulch. Just by that one question, I made friends with my "weeds," and now see them as important members of my gardening family (weird, huh?). Of course, there are still some weeds that are black sheep (I'm looking at you, crabgrass), but I know even those do some good (ground cover, for instance). I list my favorite weeds in Chapter 6.

Other questions that could make a difference in your garden (and life):

"What are my reasons for gardening?"

"How much time do I have to have to dedicate to my garden?"

"What are my physical limitations?"

"How dirty do I want to get?"

"What does my family eat (or would they be willing to eat)?"

"Can I have a garden close to my house, or will it be farther away?"

"How well do I handle failure?"

"How will I use the vegetables I grow?"

"Will I enter any produce into the fair?"

"How early in the season can I plant this vegetable?"

"Why did some plants survive the frost and others didn't?"

"How much shade do I have in my yard?"

"Should I learn to can?"

"What happens when I save hybrid seeds?"

"Why is this vegetable so difficult to grow?"

"Can I grow vegetables in the front yard?"

If you believe the Internet (and who doesn't?), you can use all kinds of "hacks" (like using Epsom salt or children's vitamins to fertilize), though I can honestly say I've never successfully used one. As Abraham Lincoln said once (according to a Facebook meme), "Don't believe everything you read on the Internet." Hacks are a really good time for your question-thinking to come into play. Ask yourself not only "Will this work?" but also "Why does this work?" Most hacks are based on scientific evidence and facts (you would hope). I think it's more important to know the "Why" than the "How." Understanding that makes you a better gardener. Don't be afraid to seek assistance if you have a problem like dead plants or unknown insects. The more you know, the better the questions you can produce.

Demand results

As you read this book, keep in mind the number one goal of every veggie gardener: production. Your goal should be to have food to eat from your garden. Some years, that may be mostly weeds. Other years, you'll have way too much produce to deal with (which is when you either learn to can or give away veggies to friends and family). I delve deeper into minimizing losses in Chapter 5. One way to guarantee success is to plant the less challenging veggies. So let's jump to Chapter 2 where we can talk about all the different vegetables and discover those that yield greatly yet easily.

Chapter 2 – All in the Veggie Family

Knowing which plant belongs to which family will help you to create your garden masterpieces. Think of each family as a different color on your palette. Using just one (like the nightshade family tomatoes and peppers) is plain boring. Be sure to splash all (or most) of these around for a full rich effect. For your convenience, I've included all these plants in a handy dandy PDF, FREE for downloading, which lists 50 plants ranked by how easy they are to grow (based on my snarky opinion of course). Utilize this tool to plan next season's veggie garden. It's available at http://thesnarkygardener.com/veggie-growing-guide.

Vegetables can be categorized into families based on genetics and similar traits. These groupings are advantageous to the food gardener. If you know one plant, you can assume certain properties of the other members. For instance, I've grown tomatoes for years, but this was my first season raising ground cherries. Though ground cherry fruit has the papery outer shell of the tomatillo (also in the nightshade family), many other traits are the same—lack of cold tolerance, seed saving techniques, need of a cage for support, and drought resistance. It's also important to know that plants in the same family are susceptible to the same diseases and pests. Planting in different places year to year (known as crop rotation) will keep your plants safer. Lastly, plant families tend to have the same nutritional requirements. I've listed 8 family groupings, though they may be known differently in scientific naming. I'm a biology layman and prefer to use more common names (silly Latin snobs).

Helpful definitions:

Annual - must be planted every year

Bi-annual - will overwinter and send up flowers the following year

Perennial - will come back year after year

Full Sun - 6 or more hours of direct sunlight a day

Partial Shade - 3 to 6 hours of direct sunlight a day

Self-pollinating - don't need other plants to produce seed, plus don't cross with easily

Open Pollinated - seeds that can be saved (unless there's been cross pollination)

Heirloom - Open Pollinated varieties that have been around for 50 years or more

Hybrid - First cross between Open Pollinated varieties. Seeds saved may not grow the same as parent

Bolting - produce flowers and go to seed, usually with lettuce and other leafy greens

Direct seeded or sown - seeds are either buried less than an inch under the soil or spread on top of the soil.

Transplanted starts - plants that are purchased from a garden store, are started by you indoors, or are started from cutting off a parent plant

Not So Helpful definitions:

GMO - Genetically Modified Organisms, uses DNA science instead of plant breeding. You can't purchase GMO seed for your garden

Hangry - when you are so hungry that you get angry

Original photo by Kara Whaley. Sketch by Carol Grzeschik.

Nightshades

The nightshade family includes tomatoes, potatoes, peppers, eggplants, and ground cherries.

Traits in common:

- Frost intolerant (potatoes can be planted before last freeze, but if the leaves are exposed to the cold they will die but will grow back)

- Heat-loving

- Full sun (6 or more hours)

- Drought tolerant

- Self-pollinating

- Easy to save seeds

- Leaves and stems are poisonous (including the green parts of potato tubers exposed to light)

- Annual in temperate climates

- Tomatoes, peppers, ground cherries, and eggplants are normally started inside (or purchased) and then transplanted outside

- Potatoes are planted using "seed potatoes" purchased from a garden store or online

- Common diseases and pests: blight, potato beetles, hornworms, deer

Snarky Gardener favorite - Tomatoes

I think tomatoes might be every gardener's favorite vegetable. I know individuals who only grow tomatoes to the exclusion of every other (don't be those people). Homegrown tomatoes taste better than anything you can buy at the store. Store tomatoes (I call them "plastic tomatoes") are grown for their ability to travel and not bruise easily. Your tomatoes will be produced for their flavor and use (i.e. paste, slicing, salads, canning).

I would recommend buying tomato plants (a.k.a. starts) from a reliable local greenhouse if you are just getting started. If you are so bold, you can start tomatoes from seed inside about 6 weeks before your last frost in the spring. Starting plants isn't overly complicated, but you will need to acquire equipment and supplies to do it properly (grow lamps, watering cans, starting soil, and pots). Try not to plant into the ground too early, since any frost or freeze will kill your tender little plants. I know spring excitement will tempt you, but there's nothing sadder than going out and finding all your babies blackened and lifeless.

To plant tomatoes, follow these steps:

With spring looking to summer, thoughts turn to planting frost sensitive tomatoes. The best time to put these little guys into the ground is when the soil has warmed up and all chance of frost has passed. Of course, one cannot tell the future, but mid-May on is generally considered safe. If you do plant and then there is a freeze or frost warning, covering the plants with straw/leaf mulch or blankets should give them enough protection.

River, my Toy Fox Terrier, digging tomato holes. Photo by Carol Grzeschik (aka the Snarky Girlfriend).

Tomatoes are special, in that their stems will grow roots if they encounter soil. Dig down enough to cover the stem up to the first set of true leaves. This will allow the tomato to receive all the water and nutrients it needs. In addition, it will be easier to cover them if the weather turns cold (being shorter and all). I usually dig my holes ahead of time and plant either on a cloudy day or in the evening to stress the plants less.

As you can see above, I use the "Terrier" digging method, but you can also use a shovel. Before placing your plant in the hole, you may want to add some extra fertilizer or other materials to the hole. Some "experts" recommend adding Epson salts, as they contain magnesium and sulfate. Others recommend eggshells with their needed calcium. I tend to use "dynamic accumulators"—plants that collect and store minerals. My favorites are comfrey (pictured below), dandelions, and mustard greens. I just remove the leaves I need and bury them with the tomato roots.

Comfrey – a dynamic accumulator

Tomato planted so first true leaves are almost touching the ground

Once planted and watered, you should add some support, whether it be a tomato cage, fence, or stake. Some tomatoes (called determinate) don't need much since they only get a few feet tall (like the Roma variety, for example). Putting in support now means you won't be piercing roots later as the plant matures. As you can see below, I make my own cages out of steel fencing. These totally surround the plant and are 6 feet tall, providing support for most varieties of indeterminate tomatoes. The other positive of this system is that peas can be grown up the cages to give more food production plus nitrogen fixing for future crops.

Steel fencing cage around the tomato plant

One other technique I stumbled upon is to grow tomatoes on the north side of an east-west steel fence (behind the caged tomato in the above picture). As the plants grow up, I weave the branches in and out of the wire, thus eliminating the need to use ropes or other bindings to keep the plant from falling over. Just be careful when redirecting the vines, as they break easily.

Tomato plant later in the season

There are two different types of tomatoes— determinate and indeterminate—so pay attention when you are buying them at the store. Determinate (otherwise known as "bush") grow with a predetermined height, usually 3 feet or so. These produce all their fruits at once, then are pretty much done. The advantage of determinate is they don't need as much support (cages, poles, etc.) as the indeterminate tomatoes. If you are going to grow tomatoes in pots, determinate is the way to go. Indeterminates produce fruit all throughout the summer until the first frost (mid-October here in Ohio). Most tomatoes (especially cherry) are determinate.

Snarky Gardener favorite - Potatoes

Yes, potatoes are cheap to buy at the store, but if you knew how commercial potatoes are grown (described in detail in Michael Pollan's book *Botany of Desire*), you'd think twice about eating them. Potatoes are easy to grow and you will taste the difference. First, buy your seed potatoes in 3 to 5 pound bags at your friendly neighborhood gardening store. Next, dig a small ditch, plant your seed potatoes eye pointing up, and then bury them with soil. In about a month, the seed potatoes will send up green tomato-looking stems and leaves. Every time the stems grow to 6 inches tall or so, mound up dirt, leaving only the top leaves showing. You can put potatoes into the ground as soon as March 17th (St. Patrick's Day), but I usually wait until April. Any green foliage that pops up is frost-sensitive and will need to be covered under leaves or other mulch if you get temperatures below 32 degrees F.

In about 60 days (give or take a few weeks based on the variety and your local conditions), you'll notice tomato-looking flowers. This means the potatoes are starting to produce tubers underground. In another month or so, the top of the plants will start to die off. This doesn't mean you should worry; it just means the potatoes are almost ready to dig up. I usually let the plants die entirely before harvesting. I've also had success with leaving them in the ground over the winter, and digging them up once the ground thaws in the spring.

Award winning potatoes

Note: There are quite a few Internet methods you will come across for growing potatoes (i.e. in bags, in old tires, in wooden towers), but try sticking to this time-honored method when starting out.

Zucchini

Cucurbita

Also known as the squash family, the cucurbita family includes summer squash (zucchini, crookneck, and yellow), winter squash (acorn, pumpkins, butternut), cucumbers, watermelons, and melons.

- Frost intolerant

- Love the heat (especially melons and watermelons)

- Need full sunshine (6 or more hours), though cucumbers like a little shade during the hottest months

- Can be planted by seed or seedlings (though tend to do better with direct seeding)

- Plant seeds in mounds to help with getting soil to a high enough temperature for germination

- Bush and vining varieties

- Annual in temperate climates

- Common pests and diseases: powdery mildew, vine borer, squash bugs, cucumber beetles, deer

- Easily cross with others in the same cucurbita sub-family—squashes cross with pumpkins, cucumbers cross with other cucumbers, watermelon with other watermelons

Snarky Gardener favorite - Zucchini

Burpee's Sure Thing Hybrid Zucchini

Zucchini has the reputation of bountiful production, to the point of gardeners giving it away to everyone who can't get away fast enough. Permaculture views this natural abundance as a good thing, since it allows you to share your bounty, building relationships and community in the process. I tend to grow seedless bush varieties, like Burpee's Sure Thing Hybrid http://thesnarkygardener.com/2015/11/07/burpees-sure-thing-zucchini-review/, as they don't need pollination. Bush zucchinis usually only produce well for the first month or so of production. To mitigate this issue, plant a few each month or so throughout the summer. Of course, you can't save seeds with seedless plants (because there are no seeds—pay attention!). Squashes cross pollinate so readily that it's difficult to keep them from becoming "Frankensquash" hybrids of pumpkins, winter squashes, and zucchini—so I don't see seedless as a problem in this case.

Alliums

Includes onions, garlic, leeks, shallots, and chives.

- Perennials - Egyptian walking onions, bunching onions, chives

- Bi-annual - Onions, garlic, leeks, shallots

- Mammals (including deer) will AVOID these like I avoid musicals and chick flicks

- Relatively pest free

- Can handle partial shade (3 hours plus of sunshine)

- Can be direct seeded but much easier with bulbs (onions) and cloves (garlic)

Snarky Gardener favorite - Garlic

Braided Soft-necked Garlic

I love garlic because it's easy, plus the bulbs you buy at the grocery store are of poor quality. Here in Ohio, they are planted in mid-October, to be pulled in July or August the following year. There are two types: soft-necked and hard-necked. Soft-necked can be braided (see *picture* above), but aren't as cold hardy as hard-necked. Just break up your saved or purchased bulbs into cloves, and plant the biggest a few inches down (and eat the rest). Make sure the plot is well drained and cover it with several inches of mulch to protect during the winter.

Egyptian walking onions

Snarky Gardener favorite - Egyptian walking onions

Egyptian walking onions are perennials that eat like green onions (the tops) and shallots (the bulbs). As they mature through the summer, they develop bulblets (several little bulbs clustered in a group) at the top of stalks. They "walk" when these 2- or 3-foot stalks fall over, planting a new set in another part of the garden. Self-planting onions—very cool. The woman I received mine from said hers walked over a hundred feet to colonize a second area (with none growing between). I still wonder how they did that (animals, maybe?). Ah, nature.

Red Russian kale

Brassicas

Includes broccoli, Brussels sprouts, cauliflower, cabbage, kale, arugula, rutabagas, turnips, mustard.

- Mostly bi-annuals, though mustard will go to seed in the same year

- Frost tolerant

- Prefer full sun but will grow in partial shade

- Produce lots of seeds

- Flowers are good for bringing pollinators into the garden

- More domesticated varieties are sweeter, but also have more pests—broccoli, Brussels sprouts, cauliflower, cabbage, kale, arugula (in that order)

- Can be directly sown or transplanted

- Pests include cabbage worms, deer, and groundhogs

- Turnips, rutabagas, and mustard are more bitter but have less issues with pests

Snarky Gardener favorite - Turnips

Able to grow in soil types of all kinds (including poor), I didn't really appreciate turnips until they were in my garden. Back in the day, turnips (and rutabagas for that matter) were famine foods. During World War I, the winter of 1916-17 was known as the Turnip Winter, because food was so scarce for the German civilians. Wet weather caused a potato crop failure, and turnips (normally an animal feed) were all that was available.

Turnips are easy to grow, especially in spring and fall, as they can handle frosts. The greens are more nutritious than the bulbous taproot, but tend to be bitter because of glucosinolate compounds produced by the plant to fight disease and pests. I find turnips will not be eaten by groundhogs, deer, or cabbage worms, whereas other brassicas (especially broccoli) will be. My guess is that the bitterness is stronger in turnips than the other family members.

Snow Peas

Legumes

Includes peas, beans, American groundnuts.

- Fix nitrogen, which means they take nitrogen (an important plant nutrient) out of the air and turn it into a usable form in the soil

- Annual (except groundnuts)

- Prefer full sun but can handle shade

- Peas can handle cold (traditionally planted in March here in Ohio)

- Bean and groundnuts are frost intolerant

- Self-pollinating

- Easiest seed to save of all the families

- Easy to grow

- Should be directly sown only (no transplanting)

- Pests include most mammals (especially rabbits)

- There are bush and vining varieties

Snarky Gardener favorite - Beans

Jacob's Cattle beans. Original photo by Kara Whaley. Sketch by Carol Grzeschik.

Beans come in two types: bush and pole. I prefer bush beans for two reasons: quick growing times (60 days or less) and no supports are needed. I tend to grow two varieties of bush beans: Tendergreen and Jacob's Cattle beans. Tendergreen produce excellent green beans, especially for canning dilly beans. Jacob's Cattle beans (so named because they are mottled like a cow) can be eaten green but are better as a dry bean for soups and chili. They take between 90 and 110 growing days before being harvest ready, as they need to be completely dry before storing.

Note: The beans you cook in a chili are also the same beans you plant. If you purchase beans at the grocery store, especially organic ones, you can use them as seed.

Spinach in the spring

Spinach

Includes spinach, Swiss chard, and beets

- Cold tolerant (especially spinach)

- Bi-annual, though spinach will bolt if heat stressed

- Handle shade well (3 hours minimum)

- Can be direct seeded or transplanted

- Pests include deer and groundhogs

Swiss Chard

Snarky Gardener favorite - Swiss chard

I didn't always like Swiss chard, but have warmed up to it in recent years. It reminds me of spinach on a celery stick. You can direct sow, but I sometimes have issues with germination, so I'll plant them inside first and then transplant when they are big enough. Swiss chard is especially heat and drought resistant and will produce throughout the summer without bolting. We usually eat it by sautéing it in olive oil or wine, cooking the stems first then adding the leaves later. Add some grated cheese (or nutritional yeast for you vegans), and you have a very delicious and nutritious side dish.

Chocolate Mint in the front yard at Snarky Acres

Mints

The mint family includes peppermint, spearmint, lemon balm, thyme, rosemary, sage, oregano, and basil.

- Aromatic (i.e. smelly) herbs

- Square stems

- Perennial (basil would be if not for its frost intolerance)

- Spread easily to the point of invasiveness (my definition of abundance)

- Handle shade well (3 hours minimum)

- Flowers good for bringing pollinators into the garden

- Provides good ground cover

- Drought tolerant

- Relatively pest free (including deer and other mammals)

- Usually propagated through cuttings, though can be started with seed

Note: In Ohio, it's probably best to pot up rosemary and bring inside before the ground freezes.

River digging amongst the oregano. Picture and sketch by Carol Grzeschik.

Snarky Gardener favorite - Oregano

Oregano is my favorite mint, though I enjoy the others too. I've been crazy enough to spread it throughout my garden. Oregano's little purple flowers bring in the bees and beneficial insects like no other plant. During the summer, my oregano plants are busy insect airports that I avoid so I don't get stung. Oregano is also one of the first plants with foliage in the spring, and it dries easily for use during the winter. In my garden, it grows so aggressively that I've had to use a push mower to cut paths.

Sunflowers

Includes sunflowers and sunchokes (Jerusalem Artichokes)

- Native to the eastern United States

- Stems of 6 to 12 feet tall

- Ants will herd aphids up them, keeping them out of other parts of the garden

- Can provide living poles for beans

- Not frost tolerant

- Drought tolerant

- Need full sun

- Plant seeds with sunflowers and tubers with sunchokes

- Pests include deer and groundhogs

Snarky Gardener favorite - Sunchokes

Sunchokes ready to be cooked

Sunchokes, also known as Jerusalem Artichokes, are like sunflowers, but instead of harvesting seeds for food, you dig up tubers in the fall through the spring. Once planted, they will probably always be with you. Even if you think you've dug up all of them, there will be stragglers. The tubers taste like a strange combination between potatoes and water chestnuts. They are filled with inulin (not insulin), which some people (including this Snarky Gardener) can't digest well, leaving them quite gassy. Fortunately for all involved, sunchokes (a.k.a. fartichokes) can be pickled or fermented to lessen or eliminate this issue.

Mache or corn salad

Lettuce and mache

- Cold tolerant (especially mache or corn salad)

- Shade tolerant (3 hours plus)

- Self-pollinating

- Bolt in hot weather

- Annual

- Can be direct sown or transplanted

- Pests include most mammals

Carrots

Includes carrots, parsley, dill, fennel, parsnips, celery, and cilantro.

- Bi-annual

- Frost tolerant

- Shade tolerant

- Flowers are good for bringing pollinators into the garden

- Can be direct sown or transplanted (though carrots should probably be directly sown)

- Pests include mammals and parsley worms (which turn into Swallowtail butterflies)

Three Sisters - corn, beans, and squash

Corn

- From the grass family

- Annual

- Frost intolerant

- Need full sun

- Pollinated by wind, will cross with commercial GMO varieties

- Direct seed only

- Heavy feeders (they take more nutrients from your soil than the average plant)

Blending the families

Putting different plant families together (referred to as "companion planting") can be advantageous for the veggie growing artist. Books like *Carrots Love Tomatoes* list out the vegetables, herbs, and flowers that can be planted side-by-side for the mutual benefit of all involved (including you!). A classic example is planting basil with tomatoes, as the basil is said to make the tomatoes more flavorful. There are also plants they say you should keep apart (legumes like beans and peas shouldn't be planted with those in the onion family, for example). You can also find lists on the Internet, though they seem to be copies of each other. My recommendation is to use companion planting as a guide, but don't take it too literally. Most of this data has not been scientifically tested; meaning, it's mostly based on observations, some of which are conflicting.

One personal funny story (to me, anyway) I have is with garlic. As mentioned above, it's supposed to be a deterrent for deer and rabbits. Because of this fact, I tend to plant it on my garden's borders, either just inside or outside my fencing. I had a really thick garlic patch on the eastern side of my garden, since that's the section farthest from my house (less human activity equals more animal activity). Walking with my dog one day, guess who we scared out of this strip? Several rabbits, of course. My explanation was them using it as cover? Don't believe everything you read (including this sentence). Consider trying out your own companions. Garden experiments are always fun, and are one of the best ways of truly learning.

Here's a real life blending example of two easy-to-grow crops. Around August 1 (about 75 days before my average last frost), I decided to start one last green bean planting for the year. Using my hoe to create six east to west furrows, I then planted beans every two to three inches (all very standard). After the beans sprouted a week or two later, I performed a quick weeding and then mulched between the beans with spent turnip stems I had gathered seeds from. Because it was impossible to harvest all the turnip seeds out of the mulch, I also ended up planting turnips. These grew underneath and around the beans. I was able to pick two harvests of beans before the first frost. The frost killed the beans, but turnips love cool weather. The dead bean plants thus made a nice mulch for the turnips (turnabout is fair play, after all). The turnips were pulled in November and December with some left behind for seed next year.

Permaculture blends plant families in an even deeper way. Companion planting tends to apply to annual plantings (examples: peas with turnips, carrots with onions). Building on this, permaculture "guilds" establish relationships between groups of plants (normally perennials) for the long term. Unlike with companion planting, there aren't many standard guilds—though I found a few online articles that specifically list them out (especially for trees). The closest standard seems to be the apple tree guild, with beneficial plants growing underneath. Usually included are comfrey (discussed earlier in this chapter), chives (to deter critters), strawberries, and other flowering plants to attract pollinating and predatory insects. I've been trying out a guild made up of sunchokes, pole beans (to grow up the sunchokes), American Groundnuts (a perennial native legume), oregano, Creeping Charlie (a weedy groundcover mint that has come along for the ride), and Asian dayflowers (another opportunistic weed). Four families (sunflower, legumes, mint, and the Asian dayflowers) working together year after year while providing lots of food and organic material. The only work I need to do is plant the beans in May and harvest the sunchokes and groundnuts in the fall (yeah, permaculture!). Guilds provide us another opportunity to experiment in our own gardens so we can discover our own special combinations.

When I first started learning about gardening, plant families really intrigued me. Discovering that turnips, cabbage, and broccoli were all related made sense and blew me away at the same time. Realizing that mint, oregano, and basil are all similar helped with planning. Even better was learning that disparate veggies could be grown together for better results (like the Three Sisters garden of corn, beans, and squash. What was common sense for our ancestors is brand new to us modern people. Hope this chapter brought you up to speed.

Chapter 3 – Permaculture Awkwardly Explained

Now that we've reviewed the vegetable plants and families, what should we cover next? Before you go all willy nilly planting these veggies throughout your garden, let's step back a minute to look at the big picture. You want to be successful, right? Maybe we should look at permaculture as a framework for designing your ultimate garden.

Permaculture is a combination of "permanent" and "culture" (though it was originally derived from "Permanent Agriculture"), and is a natural pattern design science. People often hear about permaculture as part of a gardening discussion and think it's a new, up and coming gardening technique (like square foot gardening or vertical gardening). Actually, permaculture is NOT gardening, per se; gardening is just one place where permaculture can be applied. Steeped in nature, permaculture applications lean toward the physical world in

69

farming, earthworks, housing, buildings, heating, cooling, cooking, food preservation, and water storage. It is also utilized for human systems, such as communities, education, alternative currencies, and computer systems design (and yes, we human beings are part of nature). Other applications include food forests and rotational grazing. Permaculture is a paradigm shift, a social movement, a different way of viewing the world, and a possible framework to build your life around. I like to describe it as "Creating abundance through nature."™

Permanence is, of course, at the heart of permaculture. Permanent is relative (as we are all technically temporary), but here it refers to designing for the generations ahead of us. Energy and other inputs are high at initial implementation, with maintenance and harvesting in later years. A system can't truly be enduring while accepting continuous inputs from the outside (fertilizer, gasoline, electricity, and money). Permaculture strives to take advantage of the more renewable on-site resources—sunlight, water, soil, leaves, wood, perennial plants, animals, manure, human labor, caring, love, humor, art, music, and ingenuity. This thinking runs counter to our society's short-term focus.

I was originally introduced to permaculture through my vegetable growing education, as gardening is a gateway drug to permaculture. As my skills and experience advanced, I sought better and more efficient techniques. Discussed in blogs, podcasts, and books (my favorite being *Food Not Lawns: How to Turn Your Yard into a Garden and Your Neighborhood into a Community* by Heather Flores), I slowly internalized the overall concepts (including the realization that permaculture does not just apply to food production). In early 2015, I advanced my knowledge further by attending a Permaculture Design Certification (PDC) course (seven full weekends of fun). A PDC sets the foundation of understanding and allows graduates to pursue careers in permaculture.

I think what really attracted me to permaculture is the systems thinking that runs throughout. As a software developer for the last twenty-five plus years (wow I feel old), I've worked with systems on a daily basis. Thinking holistically is natural for me, as is resource-intensive new development versus the small tweaks of the maintenance cycle. Patterns are also a part of software development—relationships between objects, standard user interface design, project management, and so forth. To me, developing a software application is the same as putting together a permaculture design, just with a different tool set (and more dirt under my fingernails).

A set of ethics guide permaculture:

1. Care of Earth

2. Care of People

3. Return of Surplus (or sometimes Fair Share: Set Limits and Redistribute Surplus).

For people looking in from the outside, permaculture seems like repurposed ancient techniques (I was told this by an experienced Master Gardener and I agree). Here's an important differentiation: permaculture is not about techniques (though some are labeled as "permaculture techniques"), but on designing deliberative systems that utilize these techniques with the three ethics intertwined. Just because you dig a swale (otherwise known as a big giant trench on contour) to hold water doesn't mean it's permaculture. If the trench is just one piece of a whole design with an understanding of water flow and storage, then it's permaculture, because intentions drive design. Just implementing a technique when it's cool and trendy is not. I've also seen examples where people have implemented permaculture-like systems (for example, the rotational grazing of Joel Salatin's Polyface Farms), but I would argue they are not practicing permaculture (not that there is anything wrong with that). Again, intentions drive design.

Along with the three ethics are the 12 Permaculture. These help put the individual into the proper mindset when designing.

1. Observe and Interact

2. Catch and Store Energy

3. Obtain a Yield

4. Apply Self-Regulation and Accept Feedback

5. Use and Value Renewable Resources

6. Produce No Waste

7. Design from Patterns to Details

8. Integrate Rather Than Segregate

9. Use Small and Slow Solutions

10. Use and Value Diversity

11. Use Edges and Value the Marginal

12. Creatively Use and Respond to Change

Outdoor Kitchen Example

Here's a non-garden, real life design example that might make things clearer (or murkier, I'm not sure). After attending our Permaculture Design Course, the Snarky Girlfriend and I decided to build an outdoor kitchen based on the Summer Kitchen pattern discussed in Peter Bane's book, *The Permaculture Handbook: Garden Farming for Town and Country*. We purchased a low cost semi-temporary 12' X 10' gazebo and built it outside our back door (within Peter's recommended 50 feet from our main kitchen). This simple (albeit labor-intensive) action turned an inhospitable grassy area into a multi-use room available 7 or 8 months out of the year. A two-burner propane camp stove (plus the propane grill we already had) lets us cook and can food outside instead of heating up our house unnecessarily. Observing that the area to the south of the gazebo receives 3 to 5 hours of direct sunlight a day, we installed a 5 X 5 greenhouse, raised beds for semi-shade tolerant vegetables (like beets and arugula), and a trellis against the gazebo for shade, privacy, and pole beans (not necessarily in that order). A homemade outdoor sink built with scavenged parts lets us wash vegetables without all that dirt walking into the house (and save the water for irrigation). When we aren't using it as a kitchen, we process seeds or just enjoy our backyard in shaded comfort.

All twelve principles discussed in this chapter are represented with this elegant solution (at a rental property, no less):

1. Observe and Interact - the site; especially sunlight, rain, and wind

2. Catch and Store Energy - canning, seed saving, resting, sunlight

3. Obtain a Yield - vegetables, seeds, meals, relaxation

4. Apply Self-Regulation and Accept Feedback - reconfiguration of tables and chairs as needed

5. Use and Value Renewable Resources - sunlight, water, plants, seeds

6. Produce No Waste - canning, vegetables, sink, compost

7. Design from Patterns to Details - patterns 39 and 42 from "The Permaculture Handbook"

8. Integrate Rather Than Segregate - all the disparate pieces as one system

9. Use Small and Slow Solutions - temporary and inexpensive pieces

10. Use and Value Diversity - different technologies and techniques

11. Use Edges and Value the Marginal - unused area next to house, gazebo's south side

12. Creatively Use and Respond to Change - adjust based on seasons and changing needs

Final Thoughts on Permaculture

The most important lesson I learned through my ongoing permaculture training (it's never really over) is that every person is a designer. Each of us has the talents and skills to build better systems (even for non-gardening applications), whether they be for just our own selves or for the benefit of all humanity. Permaculture gives us the tools to create these systems eloquently, using nature's gifts instead of with the finite resources of billions of years of stored sunlight in the form of fossil fuels. It is just up to our imagination and persistence to make it happen.

Chapter 4 – Permaculture for Your Garden

"Gardening is a gateway drug to permaculture." - Don Abbott

Now that I've explained to you that permaculture is not gardening, let's make things more confusing by applying permaculture design to your veggie garden (I'm sadistic that way). Applying the twelve principles from Chapter 3, we will begin with the first principle and work our way through to number twelve. Don't worry, I'll be with you the whole way (unless I get an email notice on my phone, then you are on your own).

1. Observe and Interact

Think of this as the "look before you leap" principle. Determine where north, south, east, and west are relative to your site if you don't already know. Look around your yard for "best place to grow vegetables" candidates. Seek the sunniest places possible, since most vegetables (especially anything that fruits—tomatoes, peppers, zucchini, strawberries, zucchini, melons, cucumbers, and corn) need 6+ hours a day of direct sunlight. You can purchase a light meter which will tell you how much sun a specific spot receives in a day, but remember that sunlight changes as seasons change based on angles, hours of daylight, and trees south of your garden. You can also watch closely and make notes during the day to get a general idea. Just be as observant as possible without assuming anything (you know what they say about ass-u-ming, correct?)

Here's a humorous story that hopefully makes my point. When I first moved into Snarky Acres, I had no experience with shade, as my previous site was without trees. My new garden had a big ol' sugar maple tree west of the garden about 25 feet away. In my first season out, I planted corn on the garden's most western side. It was mid-summer before I realized the northwestern corner receives shade starting around 2 PM every day. With the sun hitting the garden starting around 9 AM or so, that is only 5 hours. As the season progressed, I could see a definite difference—the shadiest spots had the shortest corn. The corn got bigger in an arc, starting from that shady corner and moving outward. Visually seeing the shade helped me discover the true nature of my garden. After that first year, I planted more shade tolerant vegetables, such as turnips, onions, carrots, lettuce, Swiss chard, and spinach there instead.

After watching your plot's sunshine, you should next observe how water interacts on your land. Note if your chosen site seems waterlogged after a rain. Is your plot at the bottom or the top of a hill? If it's at the bottom, you might need to either move up the hill or build raised beds (or hilled rows). If you plant in the middle of the hill, you will want to create your rows "on contour," or left to right as you look up the hill. This will help to slow down your water to soak in instead of having all your soil erode away.

As you are observing your site, look for signs of animals. If you see rabbits near the site, you'll need fencing unless you don't want to grow beans or peas. If you see groundhogs, observe where they live. You don't want to make the mistake of building them an all-you-can-eat buffet (been there, done that). If they are just visitors (living 50 feet or more away), build a fence to keep them out. Otherwise, I'd recommend trapping, either by you or a professional. What you do with them after that is your business. I had to tell the Snarky Girlfriend they were being taken to the upstate groundhog sanctuary (she LOVES groundhogs). I don't think she believed me, but I really didn't know what the service was going to do with them (deniability has its advantages). If you have spotted deer or find deer tracks, you'll also need a fence. I'll talk about fencing more in Chapter 5.

If you don't get the chance to discern how sun, water, and critters act on your property, your best plan is to slow your roll (is that what all the cool kids say these days?). Plant just a few of your favorite plants from Chapter 2. Maybe you could go with more shade tolerant veggies at first. Or you could use my FREE PDF to pick the first ten or twenty plants http://thesnarkygardener.com/veggie-growing-guide/. These are the easiest to grow (based on my humble yet snarky opinion). If you think you have herbivores (aka plant eaters), put up a fence around the most vulnerable (beans, peas, broccoli, and carrots). Remember, "Observe and Interact" is not a one-time event. You should do it in your life every day.

2. Catch and Store Energy

Energy storage refers to any type of energy, but mostly it's the sun's rays we store with our gardens. Plants convert sunlight into sugar, which they store in their leaves, fruits, and roots. While much of your garden will provide on-demand subsidence, plenty can be "put up" or stored. Tomatoes, peppers, cucumbers, zucchini, and others can be canned. I especially love "dilly beans," which are pickled green beans (even won a blue ribbon at the county fair for them). Potatoes, Jerusalem artichokes, turnips, onions, cabbage, and other root vegetables can be stored in a cool place like a root cellar, a basement, or even overwintered in the ground.

Another way I store energy is through my yearly fall leaf sweeping ritual. With my riding lawn tractor, I mow up my oak and maple leaves and then use a lawn sweeper attachment to collect them. This chopped up organic material (which is a mix of dead leaves, grass, acorns, and small sticks) is then dumped in and around my garden. Over the winter, some of the material will break down into compost. I utilize the remainder as mulch to hold water and keep down the weeds. Leaves are also filled with nutrients and do a nice fertilizing job.

Saving seeds (especially tomatoes http://thesnarkygardener.com/2014/09/01/how-to-save-tomato-seeds/ and peppers http://thesnarkygardener.com/2014/01/11/how-to-save-pepper-seeds/) is a great way to store energy, since they encapsulate the DNA of a new plant.

3. Obtain a Yield

Of course, the purpose of having a garden is to receive food for all your work and effort. Your first year out will probably be your hardest. In order to "obtain a yield," you might want to consider my listed top ten veggies. Greens beans (if properly protected from rabbits), zucchini, turnips, potatoes, tomatoes, and radishes should all produce well in the initial season. Others, especially perennials, may take a few years before you see results.

One more fun fact: many of our common herbs and weeds have medicinal properties. I'd list some examples here, but I'm not a doctor (not even close). As always, feel free to Google for more information.

Another yield you will get immediately from your garden is exercise. We Americans pay boatloads of money to purchase gym memberships that we only use once or twice. The garden is your on-location workout arena. My favorite "getting buff" activities are digging holes, raking beds and leaves, walking my dog, and using my broadfork (shown below). Every spring I have to work hard to get myself back into "gardening shape."

The Snarky Gardener using his broadfork to break up compacted soil. Picture and sketch by Carol Grzeschik.

One garden dividend you might not know about is mental health. The garden is an excellent green space to relax in if designed correctly. Of course, you'll have other colors besides green, especially if you plant flowers along with your veggies. My favorite flowers are purple coneflowers, sunflowers, sunchokes, violets, oregano, and yellow brassica flowers. All of these will bring in a plethora of insects, especially bees and other pollinators. And working in the soil has scientifically proven health benefits. So feel free to get dirty and enjoy the beautiful natural setting of your garden.

4. Apply Self-Regulation and Accept Feedback

This applies to the perennial systems you put in place. They tend to be much more self-regulating. You should be able to plant once and manage after that. The feedback from this might be in the form of watching how your perennial plants are doing and fixing any problems. For example, you'll need to split out chives or mint after a few seasons.

5. Use and Value Renewable Resources

Look around your residence (both inside and out), and think about what resources are renewable. Water falls from the sky. Wind blows through your yard. Food scraps accumulate after you prepare meals. Leaves fall from the trees. Tree and bush trimmings fall down to the ground. Animal manure (but not dog or cat) piles up. Sunlight shines on your roof, trees, and yard. Your plants produce seed, fiber, leafy greens, fruits, and roots. All of these are renewable and should be valued. The more you can reuse your onsite resources, the better your garden will be.

6. Produce No Waste

Waste is another word for "unused resources." Try to reuse waste with your imagination engaged. Ask yourself, "How can this item I'm about to throw out be used?" For instance, cardboard (the non-colored kind) can be used to smother weeds. Add layers of organic material on top in the fall, and by next spring, you'll have beautiful soil to plant into. This process is known as "sheet mulching" or "lasagna gardening." I'd discuss it more here, but there are way better descriptions on the Internet or in books like *Food Not Lawns*.

7. Design from Patterns to Details

Patterns are everywhere in nature. Have you ever noticed how the top (the branches) and bottom (the roots) of trees look identical? This branching repeats in many places and can be duplicated by humans in places like the layouts of our garden paths. Nature rarely has straight lines, but tends to produce in curves. I used to feel bad that I never could get my rows exactly straight, but realized later on that is because I'm part of nature—strictly 90-degree corners are unnatural. Circles, webs, honeycombs, and spirals also show themselves in the non-human world and should be embraced. Another pattern I copy from the wild is letting my plants intermingle. As long as nobody is being overshadowed completely, I let my veggies grow together to form infinite combinations.

8. Integrate Rather Than Segregate

In designing your garden, you need to make a concerted effort to blend your plants as we discussed at the end of Chapter 2. Integration of plants and features helps to produce a more robust solution. Pests love to see a nice straight line of their favorite foods; move plants around to confuse them.

You will also want to integrate your design features. Consider flow and proximity when developing your overall property layout. For instance, you may want to keep herbs close to your kitchen, since nobody wants to travel too far away when in the middle of cooking dinner. Another example is the outdoor sink. Washing your soil-covered vegetables outside keeps the dirt from moving inside and allows for easy reuse of the water for irrigation.

9. Use Small and Slow Solutions

This is one of my favorite principles, and one that we often forget or ignore. People (including me) get overly excited and will go full force when putting in a garden. If you are just starting out, or are growing a specific vegetable for the first time, use a trial first. Start with two or three plants to see how they do. You can always increase production next season when you know what to expect. I believe this is extra important when you don't know what a veggie tastes like. Maybe buying some from the store first is a good idea.

10. Use and Value Diversity

Diversity is important to the gardener. Using a large number of different plants and families, you are guaranteeing success and abundance. Every season provides us with unique challenges and opportunities. One year might be cold and raining (like 2014). Another might be really rainy at the beginning and then droughty the rest of the season (looking at you, 2015). As you probably could tell from Chapter 2, plant families have preferred conditions. Nightshades and cucurbits like the heat; brassicas and spinaches prefer the cool. Mints like moist conditions; nightshades, not so much. The bottom line is to cultivate a variety of vegetables to ensure you'll have something to eat. And remember, weeds are by definition resilient, and many are edible. I've had times when weeds were my only produce (sad, but true).

11. Use Edges and Value the Marginal

In permaculture, the edge refers the space where two different environments meet. The classic example, and one I see on a daily basis, is the edge between woods and field. Snarky Acres is bordered by woods on the north. The plants on that edge are more diverse than that of either the woods or my yard. I see plenty of brambles (multiflora rose and raspberries), ivy (especially poison— itch, itch, itch), trees of all kinds and sizes, and other "weeds" (including my favorite, garlic mustard). This edge is also where wild animals tend to travel—based on sightings, discovered tracks, and sounds I've heard.

Garden fencing is another great example of edge. Instead of viewing it as just a barrier to entry, I value it as a place to grow my veggies. Outside the fence, I plant aromatic vegetables such as garlic, chives, mustard, turnips, thyme, sage, oregano, rosemary, lemon balm, leeks, and onions. If you remember from Chapter 2, the animals that roam my property rarely disturb these. On the fence's inside, I grow plants that are vulnerable when young (like tomatoes) and need support later in their lives. One trick I've developed over the last few years is to guide the tomato vines through the fencing as they grow up. This allows the tomatoes to remain upright without having to use ties or ropes. Another benefit of fencing is it's a place where materials accumulate. Throughout the year, birds will perch on the fence before jumping down into the garden to eat bugs and slugs. In addition, their droppings help to fertilize the area. In the fall, leaves gather, making an automatic mulching for the perennials for when they winter over. Gotta love the edge!

12. Creatively Use and Respond to Change

"It's not the strongest of the species that survive, nor the most intelligent, but the ones most responsive to change."

- Charles Darwin

Change is inevitable with your garden. Weather patterns are getting weirder by the year. New neighbors move in and start using chemicals on their lawn. Your plants aren't growing as well as you thought they would. New garden pests are eating your stuff. Planning is important, but don't get stuck on the plan. Plans are meant to be changed.

Other permaculture concepts and principles:

"The Problem is the Solution"

This is one of my favorite permaculture sayings. The standard example is the gardener who complains they have too many slugs in their garden. The answer is "You don't have enough ducks," as the ducks will eat slugs without bothering the plants too much.

My personal illustration is the attitude I have toward weeds in Chapter 1. Instead of complaining about weeds taking over my garden, I analyzed what they were and how I could exploit them. I took my problem ("Stupid Weeds!") and made it a solution ("More food to eat, plus ground cover"). Turning our perceived problems on their heads is using some of our best human traits to its fullest—creativity and ingenuity.

Soil Food Web

Another important concept in permaculture and every garden is the "Soil Food Web" http://www.soilfoodweb.com/. This is the top six inches of your soil's ecosystem. Made up of protozoa, bacteria, fungi, nematodes, insects, and worms, this environment spells the difference between a healthy successful garden and a poorly performing one. Traditional gardening and farming tills the soil, which removes the "weed problem" in the short term but disturbs this delicate system by mixing up the soil's structure and killing valuable flora, fauna, and especially fungi. In addition, with tilling, you bring up weed seed from years past that are just waiting for the opportunity to drive you crazy.

"How do I garden without tilling?" you ask. Hand tools—mainly broadforks, rakes, weeders, and hoes. In most cases, tilling is unnecessary to plant vegetables, as long as you keep from compacting the soil with your feet or machinery. For green beans, for example, I just pull a hoe, weeder, or stick through the soil to create furrows, pop beans in the ground, then hoe over the seed. For some, like carrots or turnips, I just scatter seed over the ground and lightly (if at all) sprinkle a thin layer of soil over them. The smaller the seed, the less it needs buried.

Another essential factor in the Soil Food Web is ground cover. You should try your best not to have bare soil unless you are planting. Uncovered soil is easily damaged by sun and water. As I've mentioned earlier, I let some weeds go wild. Creeping Charlie is great for covering soil, and easy to remove when you are ready to plant. Mulching is the other primary way I keep my soil covered. The harvested leaves (in principle 2) are utilized throughout my garden, especially in my walkways and when planting fall garlic. This organic material is broken down by the little soil critters (especially mushrooms and earthworms) and turned into wonderful in-place compost. I'm always amazed by how my fall leaves just magically disappear during the summer. I wonder where they go.

Cover cropping is a process used on farms of all sizes (including your own). This is planting not for food production, but to facilitate soil fertility and protection. Cover plants include clover (red, white, and crimson), oregano, radishes, mustard, turnips, buckwheat, and the aforementioned Creeping Charlie. Some of these will die off with the first freeze (like mustard or radishes), and others will need to be removed or cut back before planting your regular crops. Therefore, if you have some bare soil, you can either let your weeds cover it or specifically sow some of these.

Function Stacking

Function Stacking is the "getting the most bang for your buck" concept of permaculture. The more functions an object has, the better your productivity will be. The standard stacking example is the fruit tree. It provides fruit, shade in the summer, wind blocking, mulching leaves in the fall, dead branches, oxygen production, and water retention/purification. That's seven different functions! Most of our garden vegetables only have one or two functions. If you look at something like garlic, it has at least three: food, medicinal, and pest control (including vampires and werewolves).

Function stacking also applies to non-living objects. My garden fencing is a good example with at least five functions. It keeps pests (including neighbor kids) out, keeps my dog in, supports my tomatoes, accumulates leaves and other debris, and gives me a place to temporarily store my tools while I'm in the garden so I can find them later. Another inanimate example of function stacking is your smartphone. Think of all the applications it's used for: Calculator, GPS, texting, Internet access, reading, videos, photography, banking, Facebook and other social communication, and playing games. Oh, and from what I've heard, some people use it to make phone calls. Pretty sweet!

Chapter 5 – Prepare for the Worst. Hope for the Best.

As a gardener, you need to prepare yourself mentally for loss. Everything in nature is conspiring to take your best-laid plans and throw them to the wind (sometimes literally). Water is ready to pour from the sky when you don't need a drop more. Drought is around the corner to shrivel up your plants and crack the soil. Insects of all shapes and sizes are ready to drop off their children on your veggies. Little mammals are sniffing the air and thinking "Dinnertime!" Your neighbors' kids are driving motorized vehicles ever closer to your side of the property. A late spring frost is just a few degrees away. Danger and disaster possibilities are everywhere.

I believe the "Five Stages of Grief"—denial, anger, bargaining, depression and acceptance—can also apply to gardening losses.

Denial:

When you first discover proof of damage, you may not want to see it. There are obvious teeth marks on your broccoli, but you think, "No big deal. It's just a little bug damage." The hole under the fence goes unnoticed. The predicted rainstorm will pass by or won't be that bad. "My plants will recover just fine from their frost damage." "I don't think they ran over anything important." The mind has ways of playing tricks on you.

Anger:

Anger is one of the reasons people spray and spread all the nasty bug-killing chemicals. They see green worms eating up their broccoli and decide, as the lord of their jungle, to do something. What they don't know is that they are going to kill good and bad bugs alike, and make it easier to be attacked in the future. And, of course, those chemicals aren't exactly good for people and other critters either. I've been lucky that even at the beginning, I knew using something like Sevin was a bad idea.

Or, people get mad at themselves. "Why didn't I do something before to prevent this? I'm such an idiot!" Or they get angry at others, "Keep your kids out of my yard, you $*#*$(@!" Or, at Mother Nature, "Damn rain/wind/cold/heat/dry/wet!". Or at little fuzzy animals, "$&#($*! Is that a groundhog in my garden? Get out you stupid %&#(($!" This stage is when calls to the exterminator are made and vengeance upon all things cute and furry is declared.

"Don't drive angry." - **Groundhog Day**

Bargaining:

"Please, Lord, just let my plants be OK." "If only I'd listened to the weather report sooner…" "Why did I leave that gate open?"

Depression:

Losses can have a devastating effect on your psyche. I've felt utterly powerless after a groundhog attack or finding my kale plants full of icky green worms. *Oh, why do I even bother?* I think after my newly planted tomatoes are blackened by frost. Part of me wants to give up and stop growing veggies all together (just a small part, though). All the effort put into these gardening activities seems to be for naught.

Acceptance:

Finally, you get it. Nature will not be fully controlled by us mere humans. Of course, not every plant is going to make it. Losses are a natural part of gardening and life (cue the clichés). Every cloud has a silver lining, in every life some rain must fall. Don't accept any wooden nickels. I do find that knowing you are not alone helps, though.

Adapting:

There is one more stage we can add. Ask yourself, "What can I do to prevent such losses in the future?" and "What other dangers am I living with that could be eliminated or at least mitigated?" These are good questions to put your mind in learning mode (yep, *Question Thinking* again). Just make sure you are ready for the answers.

Remember, your failures mean you are learning. Every one of my failures has made me a better gardener, so learn to embrace your mistakes. I've made lots of errors in judgement over the years, including:

1. Purchased plants because they sounded cool, not because they fit in my overall plan

2. Planted too early; lost plants to frost

3. Planted too late; lost plants to frost in the fall before they could produce

4. Watered too little

5. Watered too much

6. Neglected plants

7. Weeded plants I wanted to keep

8. Stepped on plants and killed them

9. Ignored obvious pest damage

10. Over fertilized (indoor plants)

Truth be told (and I'm trying my darndest to tell the truth here), you will lose some of your veggies. I found this out the hard way over several years of dealing with my arch nemesis, the evil vicious mean hateful groundhog (otherwise known as land beaver, whistle pig, ground piggy, woodchuck, overstuffed squirrel, varmint, and destroyer of all things yummy). They love broccoli more than anything else (at least, that's my story). Fencing will not keep them out definitely. They don't have springy deer legs, but what they lack in jumping ability they make up for by digging under and climbing over (wow, I really dislike groundhogs!). Best advice here is putting chicken wire on the ground attached to the outside of the fence (an idea brought forward to me by the Snarky Girlfriend). After a few months, grass grows through the fence holes and keeps digging under to a minimum.

Of course, if the mammals don't get your greens, the bugs will. Those sought-after broccoli plants are also preferred by the white cabbage moth, those white moths you see flying around the garden with a spot (male) or two (female) on each wing. If you see little green worms eating your brassicas (cabbage and broccoli family), that is them. You can try covering your plants with row covers or applying bT (a biological pesticide) or diatomaceous earth, but I've come up with another strategy—avoidance via plant selection. Between the cabbage worms and the groundhogs, I stopped growing broccoli completely. I couldn't emotionally take the losses any more.

I have discovered some brassicas are more resistant to predators than others are (as discussed in Chapter 2). Turnips and mustard greens are rarely attacked, as their bitterness tends to be stronger. In my yard, turnips grown outside my fencing rarely show signs of major damage (except for the lawn mower). Kale is hit sometimes by the worms, but not as bad as with broccoli or cabbage. It's easier if you have chickens, as picking off all the worms will feed your flock. I've also read that the red brassica varieties make hiding harder for these worms, and predators will have an easier time finding them.

Another insect I have experienced is the flea beetle. They are tiny black bugs that make a whole bunch of tiny holes in your leaves. They will do damage to many plants, but most can handle it, so unless you are trying to go pro (farmers' market or county fair), you should be fine. Flea beetles seem to love eggplants the most and I've lost whole plants that way. One note here is that these lost plants were the weakest of the bunch. The healthier the plant, the better they can fend off invasions all by themselves. Even though humans have taken some of their natural defenses through selection for deliciousness, plants usually can fight the good fight if operating at peak efficiency.

The cold is another concern for the gardener. I'm like a ninja weatherman with my knowledge of the current 10-day forecast. In the spring and fall, I'll pull up the latest data and do a quick scan of the lows, looking for anything below 39 degrees F. Yep, not 32 F, but anything in the 30s. No matter how advanced our technology is, localized weather can still surprise us. The magic formula seems to be lows in the mid-30s and a clear cloudless sky. Clouds hold in warmth, and without them, temperatures could plunge and give you a nasty surprise in the morning. Some plant families (like the nightshades) are especially sensitive, and even if they are not killed, they will be slowed down and possibly stunted. This is a good reason not to plant too early in the season. The excitement of the spring (here in Ohio it's late April into June) causes gardeners to put tomatoes, eggplants, and peppers in the ground a few weeks too early (including little old me).

Based on what we covered in Chapter 2, each family has its own special relationship with seasonal temperatures. Some actually like the cold—especially the brassicas, the spinaches, peas, and many lettuces. Others hate the freezing mark and will not do well even in the 40s and 50s. These include nightshades (especially peppers), squashes (primarily melons and watermelons), sunflowers, and most beans (except fava beans). Of course, some don't love a good chill but will tolerate it like the mints and onions. I always find it fascinating to see what plants survive after a frost or even a good freeze. Most people see the first frost as a major event, signaling the end of the growing season, but there is plenty of stuff growing in my November and December gardens. For me, going out and seeing turnips, onions, sage, thyme, cabbage, spinach, beets, Swiss chard, and lettuce (especially my favorite mache) thriving in the late fall does my heart good. For these hardy vegetables, the cold just thins out the resource competition of the other frost-intolerant plants.

Heat too enters this discussion. Heat-loving plants will take off when the temperatures get too warm for others. Watermelons, okra, peanuts, melons, and peppers will especially appreciate warmer temperatures over 80 degrees. Some, like tomatoes, need the nights to be a little cooler or they will not ripen. On the flip side, the natural response for cool weather plants (lettuces, mustard, spinach) is often to "bolt," meaning to send up flowers and go to seed. Once you see flowers on these, you will notice that the leaves turn bitter. It's time to plant something else in their place (known as succession planting). Or you could just let them continue and collect the seeds later (yeah! free seeds).

One important design component of any garden should be fencing. For one, it keeps critters out, both mammals and humans. I'm not saying it is foolproof, as nothing really is, but a good fence will go far in deterring predation. I usually go with 5-foot tall steel 50-foot rolls found at any big box store. Five feet isn't enough to keep out deer, as they can jump up to 8 feet from what I've read. So far, the only time I've had deer in my fenced garden is when I left the gate open. If you have deer incursions, there are three ways you can go: taller fence, garlic clips, or a second fence. Taller fence can be accomplished by adding extensions to your current posts and string or barbwire strung between. For the extra fence, it would go several feet out from the first fence. With eyes on the sides of their heads, deer can't judge distance and supposedly won't jump over. Garlic clips should be installed at deer nose level every foot or so, as it's said that they dislike the smell. For groundhogs and rabbits, you'll want to add small chicken wire to the bottom, making an L against the bottom of the steel fence and the outside lawn. Grass will grow through wire, holding it in place and making the chicken wire eventually disappear.

*My Toy Fox Terrier River. Photo by Carol Grzeschik (aka the
Snarky Girlfriend).*

Fencing also has other uses in the garden. In permaculture, we call this "function stacking." Not only does a fence keep out animals, it also keeps them in. My dog River, fifteen pounds of ferocious Toy Fox Terrier, will pretty much run away and go on hunting missions if not properly leashed. The fenced-in garden gives her a place to run off all her pent up energy. Unsupervised, she'll dig up my beds looking for prey, but I just try to think of it as micro-tilling. The fence also serves as a place for tomatoes and other plants to climb. I routinely weave my indeterminate tomato vines up through the rectangles as the plants grow through the season. The support the fence gives is better than most other tomato cages I've tried over the years.

I believe the best defense for garden loss is summed up in two of the permaculture principles: "Observe and Interact," and "Respond to Change." Even during the middle of growing season (July and August), I try to get out to the garden once every other day at least. I do "rounds" (also known as "managing by walking around") both inside and out looking for signs of damage, usually while harvesting produce. It's next to impossible to visit a garden without returning with your arms full of vegetables. (I really need to remember to keep bags with me when on patrol). I found a tomato hornworm munching on a plant this way by noticing some unusual grazing on just one tomato plant. So pay attention while spending time in your garden and keep an eye out for anything out of place.

I often take River with me, getting in a walk while spreading doggy scent all over my property. She'll sometimes find a rodent hole and just dig up a storm (SO adorable). That lets those groundhogs, rabbits, chipmunks and moles know there is a vicious predator is in the area. Of course, spreading human urine will do the same thing. For some reason, wild animals don't really like us (because they are so delicious). A dog can be a real good ally if used properly. Unfortunately, River will kill the occasional mole or baby bunny. There is nothing sadder than that one little squeak before complete quiet. Terriers being terriers, I guess.

"Integrated Pest Management" is a term used in agriculture that applies to gardens of all sizes. This refers to a systematic effort to keeps insect pests in check. Your garden, if designed properly, should be a micro ecosystem with a complete food chain. Once in place, you will witness a live National Geographic documentary. I know I'm doing things right, as I'm constantly startled by little hoppy amphibians. Toads and frogs are regular residents, even though I've made little effort to provide water sources. If I sit 20 or 30 feet away from the garden, I will see plenty of birds making regular stops (usually robins in my part of the world). Usually they perch on the fencing for a minute then drop down onto the ground. They eat all kinds of creatures, including bugs I don't want there, plus leave extra nitrogen rich fertilizer. Every year I let my oregano flower, which brings in both pollinators and "good" bugs that eat "bad" bugs. It's a regular jungle out there!

Yes, loss is tough, but you can mitigate it if you plan accordingly. Here's one more idea to get you through it. Plant a wide variety of vegetables (in different plots if possible) and more than you think you need. Every season is going to be different. One year it will be rainy and cool all summer (like 2014), and the next it will be REALLY rainy in June and then droughty the rest of the year (2015). Weather variances will mean some veggies will thrive and others won't produce.

In a best-case scenario, you will have excess and can either give it away or put it in long-term storage (freezing, canning, or drying). Worst case, your garden will produce something. You may not have tomatoes, but you will have zucchinis. Your corn might be attacked by raccoons (they love the stuff), but your green beans will still be available. Weeds may take over from neglect, but those same weeds might be edible. Spreading your risk is a strategy that works both in the garden and in life.

In conclusion, as you garden, you will have some sad days. Don't let setbacks stop you from being successful. Allow yourself some time to let your mind process and go through the stages of grief. Learn what you can, adapt, and then move on. Remember, gardening should be fun. If it's not, you are not doing it right.

Chapter 6 – Edible Weeds

Looking at my garden, one would think I don't do enough weeding. That is on purpose, because most of my weeds are edible (not to mention beneficial to my garden's productivity and soil quality). Many of the plants others call "weeds" were brought to Northeastern Ohio via Europe or Asia as culinary herbs or vegetables. I also admire these plants for their ability to survive the harshest conditions (including human poisons). I wish my regular garden plants had the same resilience. Below is a list (in order of deliciousness) of some plants that will turn your weeding chores into simply picking dinner!

Garlic Mustard (*Alliaria petiolata*)

One of my favorite weeds in my backyard, garlic mustard comes up early in spring and is ready to eat by Earth Day (April 22). Though environmentalists and naturalists classify it as an invasive species, this plant is actually a culinary herb. Garlic mustard is not related to garlic, but instead is a mustard variety that tastes like garlic. It originates from Europe and has no natural predators in North America (except for the Snarky Gardener).

Best way to eat Garlic Mustard: Garlic Mustard Pesto with pasta and cheese http://thesnarkygardener.com/2014/04/23/garlic-mustard-pesto-for-earth-day-2014/.

Lamb's Quarters (*Chenopodium album*)

Lamb's quarters are closely related to spinach and beets, and are in the same family as quinoa. I found this in my yard last year, saved some seeds, and tossed them into my garden. The plants I found almost didn't make it, as the friendly neighborhood groundhog seemed to prefer it over other things in the backyard.

Best way to eat lamb's quarters: same as spinach

Violet (*Viola sororia*)

A perennial, violets not only show up in my garden; they are also spread throughout my yard. I didn't know until last year that they are edible, but have been eating them ever since. The leaves are pleasant and remind me of spinach. Like many leafy greens, the earlier in the season the better.

Best way to eat violets: leaves and flowers in salads

Plantain (*Plantago major*)

Also known as white man's foot, plantain is a yard and garden staple. It loves compacted soil, so you'll notice it growing near a lot of foot traffic. The leaves are full of nutrients with a spinach-like taste. Plantain can be used medicinally for bug bites and scrapes.

Best way to eat plantain: same as spinach

Dandelion (*Taraxacum*)

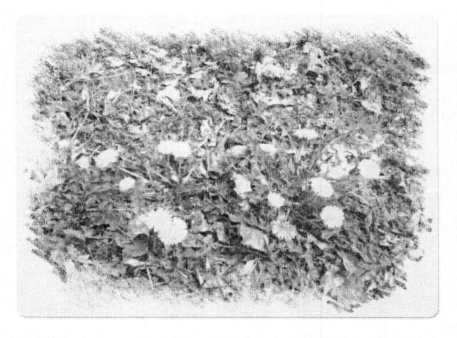

We all know the good old dandelion. I laugh when people talk about eradicating them from their yards. Not only can they be eaten, but they also help in other ways. The yellow flowers give bees pollen early in the season when they need it the most. Their long taproots bring up minerals and nutrients that are then utilized by your garden plants. Just hoe the plant down at soil level and use the leaves as mulch around your veggies. Don't worry—the taproot stores plenty of energy and will help the plant grow back in no time.

Best way to eat dandelions: young leaves in salads, flowers in fritters, and roots in beer or wine

Quickweed (*Galinsog parviflora*)

This weed took me three years to identify, as it's not common enough to show up online easily. One season back a few years, after my last full garden tilling, this plant bolted like a banshee (is that a phrase people use?) and promptly took over my garden (thus the quickweed name). Wish I would have known it was useful in salads back then. I would have had a delicious summer instead of an endless weed battle that I eventually lost.

Best way to eat quickweed: in salads

Purple Dead Nettle (*Lamium purpureum*)

In the mint family, purple dead nettle is a bee favorite. It comes up early and often on bare ground in gardens during the spring. As a salad addition, the taste isn't the greatest, but a few flowers at a time doesn't hurt too bad.

Best way to eat purple dead nettle: just a few flowers in salads

Ground Ivy/Creeping Charlie (*Glechoma hederacea*)

Ground Ivy or Creeping Charlie is a ground cover in the mint family. It's not my favorite food, but the bees seem to love it. Ground Ivy's little purple flowers give plenty of nectar to small native insects. Its strong, mint-like flavor makes ground ivy a good companion plant and natural mulch.

Best way to eat Creeping Charlie: in tea

Chapter 7 – The Gardens of Snarky Acres

Summertime backyard at Snarky Acres

By this time, you are probably curious what the gardens are like at Snarky Acres. To be blunt, they are not your normal idyllic gardens you see in magazines. Sure, there are plenty of edible plants growing at my urban homestead, but they are wilder than most people are used to seeing. As I mentioned in Chapter 1, weeds are a normal occurrence in my plot, but not in an "outcompete my vegetables" sort of way. I value diversity in my garden and make use of my "marginal" plants. In Chapter 2, I mention Asian dayflowers and Creeping Charlie as members of my example guild. Both of those just showed up, as weeds often do. I could go out of my way (and expend unnecessary resources) removing them. Instead, both are technically edible, with Asian dayflowers being quite tasty as a salad green.

Don't get me wrong: there are weeds I will remove. These are mostly from the grass family—crabgrass and the like. Again, I don't go overboard trying to totally eliminate them, but I pull them whenever I see them, especially if they are going to seed. As I mentioned in Chapter 3, protected soil is better than bare, even when covered with less desirable plants. When I put in a bed of beans or potatoes, I will pull out all the weed cover (in the form of Creeping Charlie and quickweed) beforehand. After all, I have to give my domesticated vegetables a fighting chance to get started as they co-evolved with us taking care of them.

Weeds have been the bane of gardeners and farmers for millennia. Maybe it's time we all embraced the wilder parts of our garden. Some weeds were brought to the New World with a purpose. A common "invasive" weed in the woods next to my house is garlic mustard (discussed in Chapters 5 and 6), brought over to the New World to use as an herb. Every year for Earth Day (April 22), I make a point of cooking up batches of garlic mustard pesto and share it with everyone who cannot get away fast enough. Other weeds, like lamb's quarters and violets, are native but not appreciated for their resilience and edibility. Incorporating weeds into your garden design is supported by permaculture principles 5 (Use and Value Renewable Resources), 10 (Use and Value Diversity), and 11 (Use Edges and Value the Marginal). What's more renewable, diverse, or marginal than common garden weeds?

Like many permaculture sites, perennials are featured here at Snarky Acres. In nature, these come back year after year, ensuring survival of the species. Annuals, on the other hand, must produce lots and lots of seed to continue on existing. Since I'm a renter, I don't go full tilt with trees and bushes, but I utilize perennials where I can. My favorites are sunchokes (aka Jerusalem artichokes), Egyptian walking onions, strawberries, oregano, lemon balm (mostly as an insect repellent), chives, peppermint, sage, thyme, rosemary, wild blackberries, goji berries, and apples from two past-their-prime trees on the property. It's extremely satisfying to "obtain a yield" every year without the effort of digging, sowing, planting, and watering as perennials tend to take care of themselves once established.

Snarky Acres' first permaculture plot was built around the principles of observe and interact (1), obtain a yield (3), small and slow solutions (9) and edge (11). I observed that a small section (three feet by ten feet) at the front of my house only received one hour of direct sunlight around noon. Otherwise, it was in complete shade from the house or received dappled and indirect light until sunset. I did some Internet research and discovered a nice list of perennial herbs that could thrive in the shade. From this list, I choose lemon balm, chocolate mint, orange thyme, and both regular and garlic chives.

After the initial year, the mint dominated the site but the others also did fine. In addition, I've planted shade-tolerant annuals to supplement the yield including turnips, kale, and Swiss chard. I rip out the mint like I do with Creeping Charlie (which has also infiltrated the bed—it's everywhere!) and then sow or transplant, like I do in my primary backyard garden. This edge, like my garden fencing, is self-mulching with westerly winds and a big oak tree doing all the work every fall.

As for my annuals at Snarky Acres, my tendency is to cultivate the ones at the top of my FREE downloadable Veggie Growing List http://thesnarkygardener.com/veggie-growing-guide/ (yes, yet another plug). As of this writing, the top ten annuals on my list are green beans, zucchini, garlic, potatoes, radishes, turnips, mustard, yellow squash, tomatoes, and ground cherries. One spring, I designed a new garden plot around the fact that it had been lawn the year before. My landlord tilled up the site for me (one of my few exceptions to my "no-till" rule), but the soil was compacted and full of clay nonetheless. I planted potatoes (known for conditioning soil), tomatoes, zucchini, garlic (planted the previous fall), mustard, turnips, ground cherries, and peppers. All did well despite a deluge in June and a moderate drought the rest of the year.

As you can see, I have embraced the 10th principle ("Use and Value Diversity") by planting a wide variety of vegetables. In any given year, the environment (rain, clouds, sun, temperatures, pests, and storms) will vary from seasons before. My overarching goal for my property is to produce plenty of edible goodness. If it means too many tomatoes and potatoes one year and an abundance of Swiss chard, zucchini, and cucumbers the next, so be it. It's also why I have a variety of "weeds" in my garden (see Chapter 6). Those will thrive when our more refined domesticated veggies will wither and die. I still remember the dry summer where I primarily had only purslane (a succulent weed) to eat until we started getting rain in July.

Potatoes and tomatoes growing in the new plot

After learning how to "Observe and Interact" through my permaculture design certification course, I came to realize my main backyard garden is at the top of a ridge. This means water will flow down to a low point two neighbors' yards over. Every time we have a large rain event, the neighbor's valley fills with water, creating a temporary pond with ducks and everything. Through my training, I understood my garden design needed to slow water down in order to spread and percolate it for later use by my plants. Fortunately, my established garden was already set up that way. My new plot, the one with all the easy-to-grow annuals, is adjacent to the old one, so it has the same sloping issue. I purposely dug trenches as I mounded dirt up onto the potatoes, knowing these holes would hold water (and sometimes trip me up—stupid holes).

Four hugelkultur mounds cover cropped with spinach and turnips

Another technique I employed to slow down water flow and store it for future use (Permaculture Principle 2 - Catch and Store Energy) is called hugelkultur. Hugelkultur http://thesnarkygardener.com/2016/01/29/hugelkultur-at-snarky-acres/ is the German term for garden beds made with buried wood. The wood breaks down over time, providing garden vegetables with nutrients and moisture (as in you don't have to fertilize and water as much, if at all). The wood does not have to be brand new, since rotted wood is actually better in some ways. This is wonderful way to "Use and Value Renewable Resources," permaculture principle number 5.

I implemented this technique by building four 8 foot (long) by 4 foot (wide) by 3 feet (high) raised beds. In general, raised beds are beneficial; they warm up earlier in the spring, keep humans (but not my dog River) from compacting soil, and allow plants better drainage. Usually raised beds are built with a frame around the soil, but my beds have no borders. After completing each bed, I cover cropped with turnips, spinach and clover to minimize winter soil exposure and loss. Hugelkultur beds are also a great place to grow cucurbits like squash, cucumbers, and pumpkins.

Butternut tree north of Swiss chard. Nitrogen fixing green beans helped the tree to grow up healthy.

Another permaculture system I've put into place is to let saplings grow amongst the vegetables. Permaculture is all about succession; nature's innate ability to go from barren soil to forest in a few short years (at least, in my part of the world). The squirrels and wind have planted several varieties of native trees in my garden, especially along the fence edge. Maples, walnuts, and honey locusts have grown up throughout the garden. Most sane gardeners would remove them either by tilling or digging, but you have to be a little crazy to practice permaculture. We have plans to someday move from this rented land and purchase a larger permanent property. Guess who's coming with us? These free trees with several years of growth.

Maples and tomatoes growing side by side

Chapter 8 – Action-Item Checklist

1. Procure a garden space. This could be your backyard, your front yard, inside your house, at a friend's house, or in a community garden.

2. Observe your garden space.

a. Watch rain as it falls and look at the ground after it stops. See where water pools, and if the ground remains soggy past a day or two. Check to see if water runs into your yard from a neighbor using chemical herbicides or fertilizers.

b. Learn where the sun rises, shines throughout the day, and sets. This will be different throughout the season with the till of the earth, and trees growing and losing leaves.

c. Observe your prevailing winds. You may need fencing or other windbreaks if it's too breezy. You may also want to check for commercial farmers in the area who spray their crops or use GMO corn (wind pollination can cross them with your corn).

d. Look at other gardens and farms close to your garden and see what they are growing (or just ask). If you want to save seeds of squashes or brassicas (cabbages, turnips, etc.), insects can easily cross-pollinate their varieties with yours.

e. Dig up some soil and check its consistency. Most of us are not lucky enough to have dark rich soil from the start. Here in Northeastern Ohio, we are "blessed" with heavy clay soil. It has the advantage of being nutrient-rich, but it doesn't let water flow through and can cause drainage problems. It takes time, effort, and resources to improve your soil, mostly through adding compost, natural mulch, and cover crops. Remember, the better the soil, the better the Soil Food Web can work for your plants.

3. Start your garden planning ahead of time. It doesn't have to be all official like the Snarky Gardener does it. Pencil and paper is fine too, even if it's just a list of the plants you want to grow. The more detailed your plan is, the more you will receive what you want. There is something to be said for spontaneity, but only if it's planned for (i.e. this section of my garden is for experiments or last minute additions). I always make extra blank spots where I can throw in last minute additions, as people love to give me unwanted orphan vegetables.

4. Procure your seeds based on your plans and wish list. Seed swaps, websites, and catalogs will provide you with an overwhelming amount of choices. Remember that seeds do have a shelf life. It doesn't mean that today they are good and tomorrow they are kaput. The general rule is that less seeds in a batch will germinate as they get older. The first year, 9

of 10 will sprout. The next year 7 out 10 will. So the older the seeds, the more you need to plant to get the same results.

5. If you are going to start your own baby veggies instead of buying starts, procure your seed starting supplies 10 to 12 weeks before your last frost. Here in Ohio, that would be the end of February at the latest. You can start cold tolerant plants this early, including spinach, Swiss chard, broccoli, cabbage, and lettuce. Peppers and eggplants will take 8 to 10 weeks to be ready for planting, whereas start tomatoes 6 weeks before your last frost.

6. Once you get into March, actual planting outside can start. Here in Ohio, it's said that we can plant potatoes, peas, and onion sets on St. Patrick's Day. I usually don't start planting peas and onions this early unless the weather has been unusually warm for the time of year. I usually save potatoes until April

through June. Once planted, they will start to grow and if the green foliage is exposed during a frost or freeze, they will die and need to expend more stored energy to regrow. So, either plant them later to avoid this or cover the green leaves with mulch when the temperatures are going to be below 32 F. I'm naturally lazy, so I chose later planting.

7. April will bring even more planting opportunities, but you are still not clear of frosts and freezes (don't let a one week warm up fool you). Spinach, carrots, beets, turnips, lettuce, carrots, and Swiss chard can be added to the previous month's plantings. Also, don't be shy about planting potatoes/peas/onions in this month. You haven't missed your window by a long shot.

8. May is the most popular time to plant vegetables, especially between May 15 and Memorial Day (the last Monday of May).

Again, you can now plant anything you could have planted in March or April. It's just more fun planting them earlier, since you can eat them earlier. The previously mentioned last frost usually happens in May, but please keep an eye out for low temperatures and frost warnings. Things to plant in May include corn, beans, cucumbers, squash, tomatoes, ground cherries, peppers, eggplants—probably in that order.

9. In June, you still have plenty of time to plant April and May veggies. You should probably stay away from the March ones (peas/onions/potatoes), as the heat of summer works against them. June is a good time to start looking for start sales, especially tomatoes and peppers.

10. July is the middle of summer. Planting bush summer vegetables like beans, zucchini, tomatoes, and cucumbers is a good idea at

this time. In addition, your fall-planted garlic should be ready to pull.

11. August and September is fall crop planting season. Cold tolerant crops like turnips, beets, carrots, lettuce, and spinach are ideal. A good place to plant these is where your garlic was in July. Make sure to keep up with watering and reaping. This is also the beginning of veggie goodness season. Lots of food will come in, including tomatoes, peppers, potatoes, Swiss chard, turnips, and ground cherries.

12. October is the saddest month for most gardeners, as the first frost will kill off your cold intolerant plants—tomatoes, peppers, squash, and cucumbers. However, you do have brassicas, spinaches, onions, and lettuces to keep you busy. Plus, it's garlic planting time.

13. November and December will slowly wear down your remaining plants, but keep harvesting. I particularly look forward to Swiss chard at Thanksgiving. I believe the reason why rosemary, thyme, and sage are added to fall poultry is because those are still available fresh while others like basil are long gone by then.

14. January and February are all about planning and obtaining seeds. Enjoy your time away from the hustle and bustle of your garden. In addition, this is a great time to take up indoor gardening, especially herbs and leafy greens.

About The Author

Don Abbott (aka The Snarky Gardener) is a gardener, blogger, author, educator, speaker, reluctant activist, and permaculture practitioner from Kent, Ohio. Professionally, he's a software developer, but spends his spare time producing food at Snarky Acres, his rented .91-acre urban farm. His blog thesnarkygardener.com assists others with growing food in Northeastern Ohio and beyond. He is also the founder of the Kent, Ohio chapter of Food Not Lawns. In 2015, he received his Permaculture Design Certification from Cleveland, Ohio-based Green Triangle.

Please contact him at thesnarkygardener@gmail.com.